Poems for the Lost Souls

Thank you for sharing beautiful words

Poems for the Lost Souls

By

Nila Phillips

Copyright

Published through Amazon Publishing

amazon.com

Copyright Year: 2023

Copyright Notice: by Nila Phillips. All rights reserved.

The scanning, uploading, and distribution of this book without permission is a theft of the author's intellectual property. If you would like permission to use material from the book (other than review purposes), please contact nila.phillips007@gmail.com. Thank you for your support of the author's rights.

The author and publisher are not responsible for websites (or their content) that the publisher or author does not own.

The above information forms this copyright notice: © 2023 by Nila Phillips. All rights reserved.

ISBN

[1. Poem 2. Poem book 3. Tragedy 4. Narrative Poetry]

Trigger Warning: A lot of these poems are based on mental issues such as depression, self harm, suicide and more.

Dedicated to the healing minds just wishing to be understood

Poetry For The Lost Souls

Trigger Warning: A lot of these poems are based on mental issues such as depression, self harm, suicide and more.

Poems For The Lost Souls

Do you ever get lonely
No, my mind keeps me company
But don't you ever get lonely?
No, I wish for silence and peace
You have to become lonely
No, I wish to go to sleep
Isn't it so lonely
If only it could be.

Poetry For The Lost Souls

Welcome Lost Souls, we'll start with the simple ones.
The further you go,
The darker the hole.

Poetry For The Lost Souls

The First Level

Poems For The Lost Souls

Writing is a release
To all these things,
Bottled up inside
Lined up on shelves
Trying to hide
But, you can't write
What you can't describe

Poems For The Lost Souls

The rain,
Reminds me I'm not alone
Yet, I feel alone
Hollow
Am I even here?
The rain
Pitters on the rooftop
Falls down leaves
Races on windows
Am I even here?
I feel so alone
The darkness of my room
Coldness of my bed
Numbness of my body
Am I even here?
The clock continues slipping time
Fast yet slow
It's nine
Then twelve
An hour between twelve and twelve o' one
Am I even here?
The house silent
Streets loud
Clouds dark
Moon dull
Am I even here?
Dear rain,
You accompany me
Fill this silence
Yet, you make me feel alone
And I have to ask,
Am I even here?

Poems For The Lost Souls

> N-O
> No
> Two letters
> One word
> One sound
> Rarely heard
> Why must it be so hard to say?
> N-O
> No
> One word:
> One that I can't seem to say
> One that will end up killing me someday
> It should be easy,
> I speak many words everyday
> So, why must it be so hard to say?
> The guilt that comes with saying it,
> It's unfair.

> I shouldn't have to wear this shame,
> Bare this pain
> That comes when I cannot say no
> When I cannot resist,
> When I can only give in
> The guilt that comes with it,
> It's unfair.
> N-O

> No
> One word,
> That takes all my guts to say
> One word,
> That'll come from my lips
> ....some day

Poems For The Lost Souls

I fear to be normal;
They ask me, "What are you scared of?"
"What is your worst fear?"
I think, and I realize,
I'm not afraid of the dark, spiders, heights,
Or even dying-
I'm scared to be normal,
I'm scared to fit in
I fear to judge people by their false reputation
Instead of who they are
I fear that I will become one of them,
That I will crave their validation
I don't want to be these people they idolize-
I want to be outside this box they made.

I will be the change,
The one that stands out,
The one that they'll hate
I'll stand by those who suffer silently in the crowds,
Help them when their down
Instead of pushing them to the ground.
People will say and do anything to feel better about themselves-
People are going to try to push me down
But, I will not give them the satisfaction of stopping me now.

Everyone lies;
To their loved ones
To their friends
May it be:
No, I didn't eat the last cookie
Or yeah, I'm fine
Everyone lies, sometimes
I lie,
You lie,
They lie,
We all lie.
I lie to those I love most,
Because sometimes I don't have the balls to say it
And sometimes I just don't want them to know.

Know what's wrong with me,
What's wrong with my mind,
What's wrong with home,
Everyone lies sometimes...
Maybe I just lie more than most.

Poems For The Lost Souls

Tonight I lay in my bed,
A ton of thoughts
Drowning life out of my mind
I barely float amongst the chaos
I barely breath amongst the water
I barely hear amongst the screams
The tide goes out,
But, I stay in the sea.
It tries to take me with it,
Tries to take me land,
Tries to save me.
But, it does nothing

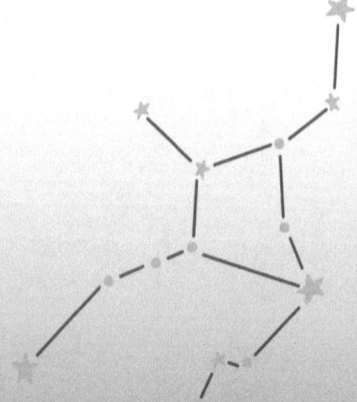

Poems For The Lost Souls

The moon has the stars
The sun has the clouds
The flowers have the sun
But, who do you have now?
Alone in your bed,

It's cold, but your covers are astray
You look up at the ceiling
Asking why you have to be this way
The trees have the leaves
The grass has the dirt
The sea has the sand
But, who do you have now since last we met?
You never meet my eyes
Put on some sort of disguise
Why can't you just tell me why?
Who do you have now?

Poems For The Lost Souls

It's not always the parents fault
Rent goes on,
Unpaid
Food isn't always,
Fresh
Clothes remain,
Dirty
It's not always the parents fault
That they get mad,
Easy
How they react,
Disarray
That they're overly,
Protective
It's not always the parents fault
That their kids treat people with,
Distaste
It's not always the parents fault
Their kids have,
Trauma
Their kids have,
Haunting memories
And, more issues than can name
It's not always the parents fault
That they don't know,
How Brokene We Are
It's not always the parents fault
What happens at school
How Cruel The Kids Can Be
It's not always the parents fault
But,
Sometimes it is.

Poems For The Lost Souls

You will never defeat me.....

You're right,
I won't
I can't defeat you
I can't defeat the never ending thoughts
I can't defeat the haunting memories
I can't defeat the past
It's part of me
I'm part of it
You're right,
I won't,
I can't,
I can't defeat the voices
I can't defeat the cravings
I can't defeat the habits
I can't defeat you..
I can't defeat you

I have no soldiers;
You have an army
I have no ammunition;
You have tanks
I have no walls;
You have a palace
I have nothing;
You have everything
How can I defeat you?
I can't

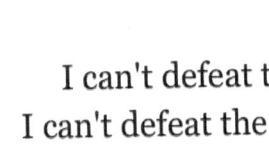

Poems For The Lost Souls

I can't seem to sleep,
My brain keeps replaying our memories
The conversations we had
The times we had
When I close my eyes,
All I see is your face
When I close my eyes,
I can see where it all took place
I can't seem to sleep.
Because, my brain won't let me forget you,
It won't let me move on past you
I keep gripping the past,
Just hoping it would last
After forever of you not speaking to me,
You sent that break up text
We went from the couple everyone knew about
To another ex
But, I can't seem to sleep
You're still on my mind..
That day if I was still there
Would you have done what you did,
Would you have ended us the way you did,
Did you even enjoy your time with me
Before you ran over me for the next?

You may have forgotten about me,
About the times we have had,
The hours we have talked,
The things we had planned,
But, I haven't forgotten about any of it;
This is all you have left me with

Poems For The Lost Souls

The water drained over an hour ago,
Yet, I stay in the empty tub
Unable to move
Unable to breath
Unable to think clearly
The water drained over an hour ago,
Yet, I don't feel like leaving
Goose bumps along my bare skin
My body numb
He asks me to get out
I keep telling him no
I don't really know why
I just can't get myself to move
The tub is cold against my skin
The air making me shiver
The water on my body already dried
The sanity already gone
The thoughts haunt me
Yet, I can't get myself to leave
I stay laying in the empty tub

If I got tested, how long would the list be?
How many things would they say is wrong with me?
Too many to count
Too many to name
Too many, yet it still wouldn't take the blame
Take the blame for what's wrong with me
For what's wrong with my mind

If I got tested, how long would the list be?
How many things would they say is wrong with me?
I can barely keep my head up some days
Barely keep the smile plastered to my face
You wanna know what's wrong with me?
Me too, I still don't know

Poems For The Lost Souls

To the little voice in my head,
I can't live without you
To the little voice in my head,
I can't die without you
Why can't you leave me be
Drifting in my mind, so lonely
To the little voice in my head,
I wish you were dead
Why can't you find something else to do instead
Let me look forward to the things ahead
Wish I could just leave you on read
But, little voice in my head,
You remain undead
Haunting me late at night instead, with your regrets
To the little voice in my head,
You've spent years with me
Locked up with only me,
Listening
Is that why you enjoy the
Torment
Because you have nothing else to do?
To the little voice in my head,
Why couldn't we work together
Why must you remind me of the past, things that never last
Why must you torment me?
To the little voice in my head,
It's another late night, sleep no where in sight

You talk to me
Reminding me of these things, I wanted to forget
Your words laced with venom
What's the point in killing me
Do you want to die that bad?
Why can't you leave me be
Do you have nothing to do instead?

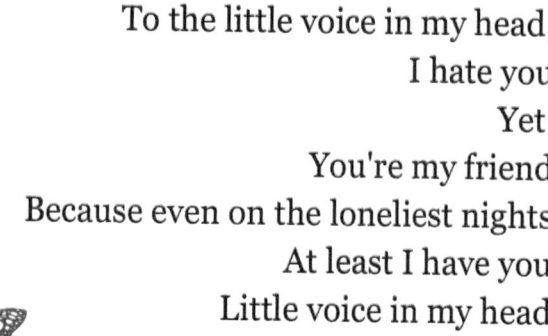

To the little voice in my head,
I hate you
Yet
You're my friend
Because even on the loneliest nights
At least I have you
Little voice in my head

Poetry For The Lost Souls

Congrats Lost Souls,

You've made it through the easiest ones,

It'll get deeper soon,

Don't fret

Poems For The Lost Souls

Maybe if I was prettier
People would like me more
Maybe if I was smarter
I would be picked more
Maybe if I listened better
I could be heard more
Maybe if I was better
They would love me more
Maybe if I wasn't so stubborn
I could accept things
Maybe if I wasn't so scared to live
I'd feel more alive
Maybe if I didn't push others away
I'd still have friends
Maybe if I was skinnier with more curves
He would be interested
Maybe if I wasn't me
I would be happy,
Finally,

Poems For The Lost Souls

I smile
You smile
This is how it goes for a while
I frown
You frown
But, do you see me
The way you think you do
Or
Do you see me
The way you want to
I falter
You go on
I crumble
You stay strong
I give in
You keep walking
I thought you saw me
But, you walked over me

Poems For The Lost Souls

You say you help me
That I need you
You don't know what I've been through
But,
You're only damaging me
With this disease
You say I can't escape without you
But,
It's you that can't escape
With or without me
You're sickened and damaged
With this disease

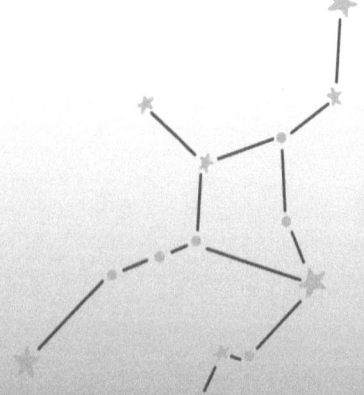

Poems For The Lost Souls

They say it gets better with time,
They say it's all fine,
But that's a lie.
It doesn't get better
It just gets easier:
Easier to hide
Easier to lie
Easier to act like its fine
The damage caused to a person stays with a person
We just hide it in the depth of our minds,
Pretend we're fine
I don't think they would like the pain
I don't think they would like that were different
I don't think they would like that were damaged
"What makes a person damaged?"
Life;
Life makes a person who they are
Life makes a person feel the pain they do
Life isn't always nice.
"But, how do you know someone's damaged?"
You don't
We hide right in front of your eyes
With our smiles,
With our laughs,
With our friends,
You can't tell were damaged
You can't tell were hurting
You can't tell it's not fine
Because it doesn't get better with time,
We just get better at hiding it.

Poems For The Lost Souls

They say you forget memories,
Ones you don't want to remember
You bury them deep
Deep
Deep
Down
Into the depths of your mind
Where only on the loneliest nights will you find
These dark pieces of you
And what you've lived through
But, this isn't true for me
I still remember,
They're not hidden behind some cloud
Hard to find
All the ones I wish to forget
Flood my mind
But, don't fret
Maybe you forgot these memories

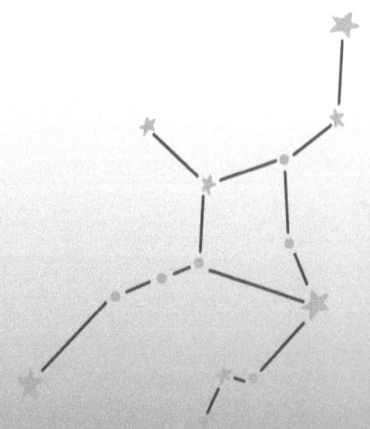

Poems For The Lost Souls

Different people understand differently,
Different people see differently,
Some relate to the pain
Some will listen to the pain
Some will distract you from the pain
But, sometimes, you can't add the weight
The weight to their shoulders
The shoulders that are already buckling
You don't want them to be more worried
To see the many more cracks that keep coming
You don't want them to worry
And offer help you can't take
Sometimes people don't see it
Or get why I do it this way
And that's okay
For me,
I switch people like seasons
So, no one ever knows everything
So, no one has that much strength over me
So, I'm never too vulnerable
But, sometimes, the person stays
Stays longer than intended
Reacts better than intended
You trust them more than intended
And that's what happened
It wasn't the plan
To get so close
To say so much
To open as many bottles
But, I did
I did with him
It wasn't the plan
But, I can't help it.

Poems For The Lost Souls

Life and death,
The one thing we all have in common
Undeniably our future
To die in some way.
Some go in cruel ways
While others simply drift away
Here I stay in life,
Wondering when death will stop by
I keep trying to call
But, he keeps hanging up
Says it's not my time
But, I'm getting tired of life
The one thing we all have in common
Death will call for us.
Who knows how we will die,
How painful or full of bliss it'll be
Sometimes good people are taken from us
And sometimes it ends suffering

I tried to call but, he won't pick up
I promise you I've had enough
Can't you listen to me now?
At least let me reach voicemail

Poems For The Lost Souls

They say I don't have anxiety
They say I don't have depression
They say I don't have eating disorders
But how would they know?
How would they know,
What goes on in my mind?
How do they know,
What happens in the late nights?
When I cry
When I want to die
How would they know?
They wouldn't.
They say I have no issues
No problems
That I'm fine
But, how would they know,
I don't want to die?
They don't know how I feel
They don't know what is real
My feelings are concealed
They would never know

Poems For The Lost Souls

Calm down they say,
That's no way to behave
Your feelings aren't valid,
Find a different outlet
You can't show emotions,
That they don't want to see
Keep the pretty smile up,
Don't conceive
You can't leave

Poems For The Lost Souls

Pain.
It changes depending on the cause
Different things hurt in different ways
But the way you hurt me,
Nothing else will feel that way
It's like a car slammed into me
Taking all my breath
Making me chest,
Tighten more than it ever has
The way you hurt me,
It will be constant for months
Trying to bite my lip to keep from crying
From all our memories
From everything reminding me
That you no longer...love me
The day you said it
That night I had a dream
Oh, such a wonderful dream of us
Now things that will never happen
Things never crossed off the bucket list
Why did you have to leave me like this?

Poems For The Lost Souls

I'm a funnel
Yes, a funnel
All the stress
The pain
The frustration
The sadness
The heartache
It all is getting poured in
While little is flowing out
It comes out so fast
I begin to over fill
Because I am a funnel
And the water
Is coming faster than I can empty

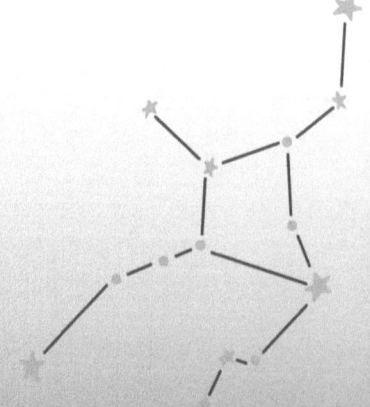

Poems For The Lost Souls

Who am I?
You'll never know
Constantly switching
Putting on a show
I'll smile wide
Then I'll wish to die
You'll never know
I'm crying inside
Not a scream
Not a shout
You'll never know me
On the inside or out

Poetry For The Lost Souls

You've completed level two,
Are you ready for more, Lost Souls?

Poems For The Lost Souls

Heart pounding
Breath quickening
Body trembling
Footsteps ascending-

I hid under the bed,
Wishing I was dead
Better than facing the man
I hid under the bed,
My stomach growling
From being under fed
I hid under the bed,
Replaying what he said
His breath against my neck
I hid under the bed,
Thinking about what I read
Now I was really dead

Footsteps quieting
Breath stopping
Heartbeat dropping
Body freezing-

What was he going to do now?
What happens in this house
Profound
What was he going to do now?

Poems For The Lost Souls

I'm messed up,
I'm stressed,
Why?
Life's fucked up
I wanna die
Why?
I hide my emotions
I hide myself
Why?
I front to everyone
Till I believe my lies
Why?
I don't let people in
I shut them out forever
Why?

I ignore my mind
I worry about others before me
Why?
I cut myself
To let the voices out
Why?

I make the water hot
To drown the screams
Why?
I lecture myself for hours
When I mess up the slightest
Why?
The same scenes play in repeat in my head
Beating me up inside
Why?

Poems For The Lost Souls

We are afraid.

We try to hide from these fears
Pretend we can't hear
The voices shouting at us
It's clear…
We are afraid

Afraid to be alone
Afraid of being authentic
Afraid to be outcast
Afraid to show emotions

Become friends with everyone
But,
Distance yourself from everyone.
Portray what everyone likes most
Put up a mask
Show everyone..

Afraid of yourself
Afraid of commitment
Afraid of rejection
Afraid of change

Eat little and turn the mirrors around
Pull away when you start to get attached
Conceal your emotions
Fight to keep it the same

Poems For The Lost Souls

Afraid of death
Afraid of silence
Afraid of putting yourself out there
Afraid to lose those you hold dear

Hurt yourself,
Stay chaotic and loud
Stay hidden in the crowd
Push them away
To make it "hurt less" when they're gone

Afraid of life
Afraid of reality
Afraid of your family
Afraid of the truth

Afraid of it all so you
Create a life in stories
Run from reality
Make family out of others
Try to escape the truth with every breath

Afraid
Afraid of ourselves.
Afraid of our insecurities.
What do we do?
Find others.
Find their insecurities
And
Fire shots at theirs.

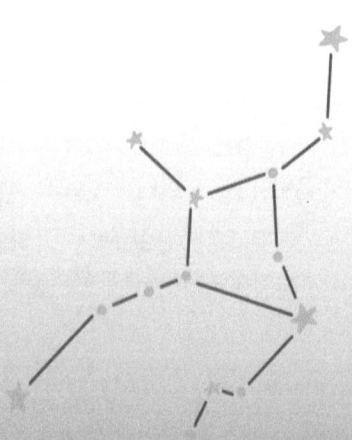

Poems For The Lost Souls

Did you hear the girl scream?
From right down the street
I heard she was chained to a wall
For all to see,
Did you hear the girl scream?
Who was only 16
I heard that you could hear her
From miles away,
Even on a stormy day
Did you hear the girl scream?
She begged for her love to flee
I heard her screams
Kept the neighbors awake,
It lasted for 6 days
Did you hear the girl scream?
Who was blamed for the murder
Of 13
I heard only one knew
She was innocent,
He was the killer of 14
Did you hear the girl scream?
Who cried out for her family
I heard her blood
Ran down the streets,
Forever guilty for the murder
Of 13

Poems For The Lost Souls

Do you know those random times
Tears fall from your eyes
When you start to cry
Those times,
When you hide in the dark shadows of your room
Wishing for the demons of depression to stop stalking you
When you curl up into a ball on the floor
All your emotion fades away
The incapability to move,
No motivation
You find no reason to keep going
No reason to still be trapped in your mind
You ask yourself "who fucking cares anymore?"
You harm yourself,
Try to end life it's self
You try the "new trend" of these days,
Suicide

Poems For The Lost Souls

But it doesn't work the way you wanted
Now your mom knows about your issues
Even though she doesn't care
She gets drunk with her boyfriend
Letting you fight these demons by yourself
Now you eat the ice cream you grabbed,
Unnoticed
You go back to the pit of hell
And sink into your phone to speak with your friends
Trying to seek the little joy you can
You're still standing here today
Maybe lost in your mind
Maybe not fully in reality
Yet you're still alive
You have not died
That is because you still have not fulfilled your purpose in life

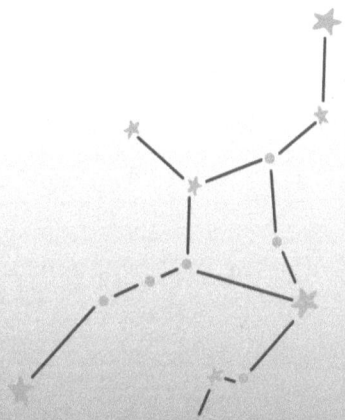

Poems For The Lost Souls

> The new trend these days
> One put to shame
> Yet everyone wants to play this game
> It can be one player
> But, let's make it two
> I'll hang my nose
> Next to you

Poems For The Lost Souls

Suicide,
Take your life
They're all thinking it
So, why not listen?
It's getting close to Christmas
Check a present off their list
It's the best gift I can give
Will you be okay with it?
I'm only asking because I'm tired
I don't know what will make you happy
The same things keep on happening
Will you stop yelling?

Suicide,
Take your life
It's an easy exit
Even if it's a temporary problem,
At least it will be fixed
Years of endurance
To build to this
I can only take so much
But, it's getting close to Christmas
I'll make it your favorite gift

Poems For The Lost Souls

Life is a complicated thing
A thing most can't understand
What is it that determines one life?
What is it that chooses when we die?
Is life set by this thing called fate
Or is it by the decisions we make?
Dear Life,
I wish to not speak to you today
You hurt me once again
So now I lay back in my familiar yet cold bed
Dear Life,
I wish to not speak to you today
It's a complicated thing
But, you left me with this off feeling
You stole my motivation and buried it under ground
How long will it be gone now?
You stole things I loved,
Said to take a break from the fun
So, life, I lay back in my familiar yet cold bed
These thoughts pondering my head
But, that's how it goes isn't it?
Dear life,
Are you lonely?

Are we simply your TV to watch when you're bored?
Do you switch between channels like people?
Do you even enjoy what you do?
Dear life,
I don't know you
I don't know what you've been through
But, you're putting us through so much
Can't we just take a pause?
I need to breathe as I'm sure you do too
So, can we call this a truce?

Poems For The Lost Souls

Dear life,
Years have passed now
I look back on what you did
I can't forget it, but I can forgive
You dug the blade in deep
Then rubbed the salt in hard
But, I will forgive
No, it's not for you
It's for me

I'm tired of looking back at these things
Dear life,
I'm finally happy
I'm not sure what it is that put you to bed
Maybe you're dying
Or simply loosening up your grip
Please don't tighten it again.
I'm finally happy
Dear life,
It's been years again
I've grown up and have my own kids,
I try to teach them of you
But, not in fear

I try to teach them to be ready for you
But, not in fear
Though you put me through so much
You brought me to this
So, life, I forgive.

Poems For The Lost Souls

Once upon a time,
Is supposed to start a fairy tale
Once upon a time,
A girl was born
Sounds good so far, right?
Once upon a time,
A girl was born
Her mother didn't care
Her father wasn't there
If it wasn't for their friends
She would be dead
Now is supposed to come the palace
Once upon a time,
A girl was born
Her parents drunks
Rent not always paid
Clothes not always clean
Food not always fresh
Once upon a time,
A girl was born
With too many issues to name
Too many traumas to name
Too many fears to name
Then the knight in shining armor
Once upon a time,
A girl was born
And she never got away
How's that for a fairy tale?

Poems For The Lost Souls

I'm not suicidal,
I just want to die
But, it only happens late at night
Yeah, I'm fine
I swear, I'm fine
My mind is not trying to kill me
No, not tonight
Did I fool you?
With my fake smile?
With my fake friends?
With my fake laughs?
Yeah, I seem fine
But, I want to die
Yeah, my mind won't shut the fuck up

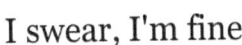

It won't leave me alone
No, not tonight
Tonight of all nights
It makes me want to scream
Cry
Cut
Die
I'm fine.
I swear, I'm fine.

Poems For The Lost Souls

There once was a girl,
Who once was innocent
Who once was okay
Then was twisted from what we call "life"
It's an awfully cruel thing
Yes, it can be nice, sometimes even generous
But why must we endure so much pain,
Before we get to see a smile on our face?
There once was a girl
Who chased butterflies
Who sang along to songs in the car
Who danced like no one watched her
Then reality hit her.
All in one sudden blow
It knocked her feet from below
Insecurities kicked confidence,
Right out the door
Trust was broken, pieces lost in the below
There once was a girl
Who had the blessing of not knowing life
Who colored pictures
And had tea time
But, then life slammed through the door.
Without knocking,
Without ringing the bell,
Without asking to come in,
And once it came,
It never left.
There's now a girl
Who is broken as the plates
Who's wishing her life to be replaced
Who's no one anymore

Poems For The Lost Souls

Screw my head for what it does to me,
During day
Through the night
The demons won't leave my side
Thoughts never ending
Happiness ceasing
Screw my head for what it does to me,
It's cruelty neverending.
Fuck the world and what it thinks of me,
I'm not perfect
I'm not loved by all
I'm not always happy
I'm screaming eternally
I'm breaking apart at the seams
I'm wishing death on me.
Screw my head for what it does to me,
Breaking me down piece by piece
Till I'm dust under peoples feet
Screw what my head for what it does to me,
Haunting, taunting me with old memories
It's like a game
A game I always lose
I'm wishing death on me.

Poems For The Lost Souls

What defines people as broken?
What causes us to get this label?
Is it the look in our eyes
The amount we cry
The shit in our lives
What makes people think they can call us broken?
Yeah, we're barely getting by
Yeah, we cry every night
Yeah, sometimes we wish to die
But, I am not broken
I am not damaged
I hold my head high
I am not afraid to act on my wants
I am not afraid of the things you say
Just know I'm not broken,
I'm not damaged,
I'm just me.
You can't label us broken,
Because we don't have shiny lives
You can't call us broken,
Because we aren't always happy
You can't call us broken,
Because life decided to hurt us
My mask is slipping,
It is cracking
But, I'm stronger than you,
Because of what I've gone through
I am not broken,
I am not damaged
And no one will tell me otherwise

Poems For The Lost Souls

A contest winning poem;
In GoodCompanyLits online first magazine

Before:
Alone
Afraid
Broken

I had no help
I had no one who understood
No one who could relate
No one who I trusted

Silence is supposed to be quiet
Then why is it so loud?
I hear my heart beat echoing
The buzzing of the fridge
The clicking of the heater
The rain pattering on the roof

Isolation can be relaxing
But to me it's terrifying
The never ending voices
Never ending thoughts

But that's before......

Poems For The Lost Souls

After:
Loved
Alive
Repaired

I have people by my side now,
People who understand
People who care
People who relate
People who help mend those cracks
No the cracks aren't completely gone
No I'm not 100%
But im on the trek of being better
Of being healthier
Of being me

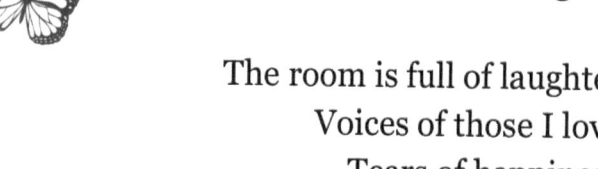

The room is full of laughter
Voices of those I love
Tears of happiness
And genuine smiles

I'm not afraid to be alone anymore
The bad memories have been replaced
The bad thoughts have been replaced
The bad habits have been replaced
A new person begins to grow

Poems For The Lost Souls

She's beautiful
But she's broken
He's strong
But he's damaged

My question is,
Why is that "but,"
Why is it not because?

She's beautiful
Because she's broken
He's strong
Because he's damaged

We're this way,
Not because of what happened,
But despite of it
We are strong
We are beautiful
And we are broken
Beautifully broken

Poetry For The Lost Souls
Authors note

Poetry is another form of art, one that holds so much meaning in simple lines. Three words on paper can say more than you ever could speak outloud, and that's part of the beauty of it.

Some of these poems are older, like a year, some are more recent. I'll be making collections of these soon, releasing one every few months. Writing gives me a sense of purpose I can't describe; and as a writer all I can do is hope to influence and connect with people through my writing.

I don't know you,

But I see you.

And that's the pleasure of writing.

I want to thank a few people for the process of this, sure it's just some poems, but at the same time it's more than that. It's the people who understood me through these times and stood by me. And the people who support my writing and are here for me everyday. They say you can't truly appreciate something till you lose it, but I can't express how thankful I am to have the people I do.

You can find me on Wattpad @Nila__Phillips

Or Instagram at @nila_the_booknerd

You can reach me by email at nila.phillips007@gmail.com

Interested in my business for authors? Check it out through my Instagram or type in this: betweenthelinescommunity.com

I have more pieces coming out in the future and I'm excited to share them with you. Don't hesitate to leave a review!